# Steve Parish™
# KIDS

# EARLY LEARNING
# BIG BOOK

# of Australian Backyards

"Your backyard has an entire alphabet and all the numbers, shapes and colours your child will ever need."

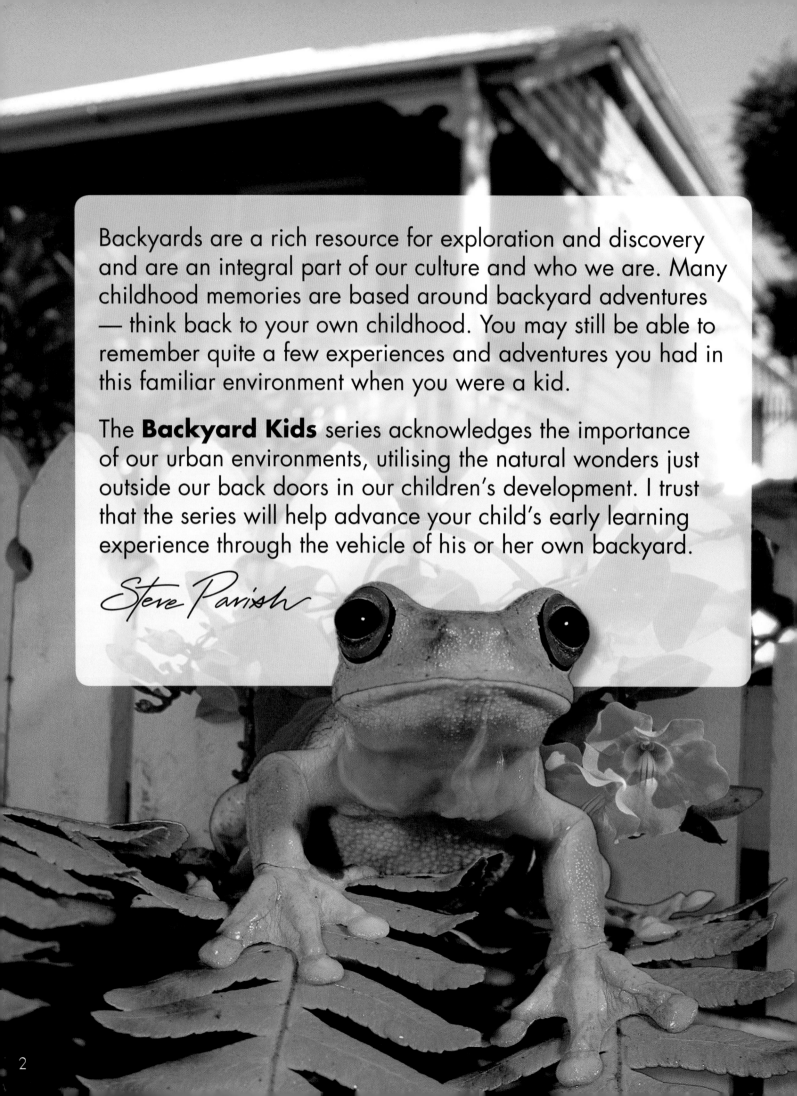

Backyards are a rich resource for exploration and discovery and are an integral part of our culture and who we are. Many childhood memories are based around backyard adventures — think back to your own childhood. You may still be able to remember quite a few experiences and adventures you had in this familiar environment when you were a kid.

The **Backyard Kids** series acknowledges the importance of our urban environments, utilising the natural wonders just outside our back doors in our children's development. I trust that the series will help advance your child's early learning experience through the vehicle of his or her own backyard.

Steve Parish

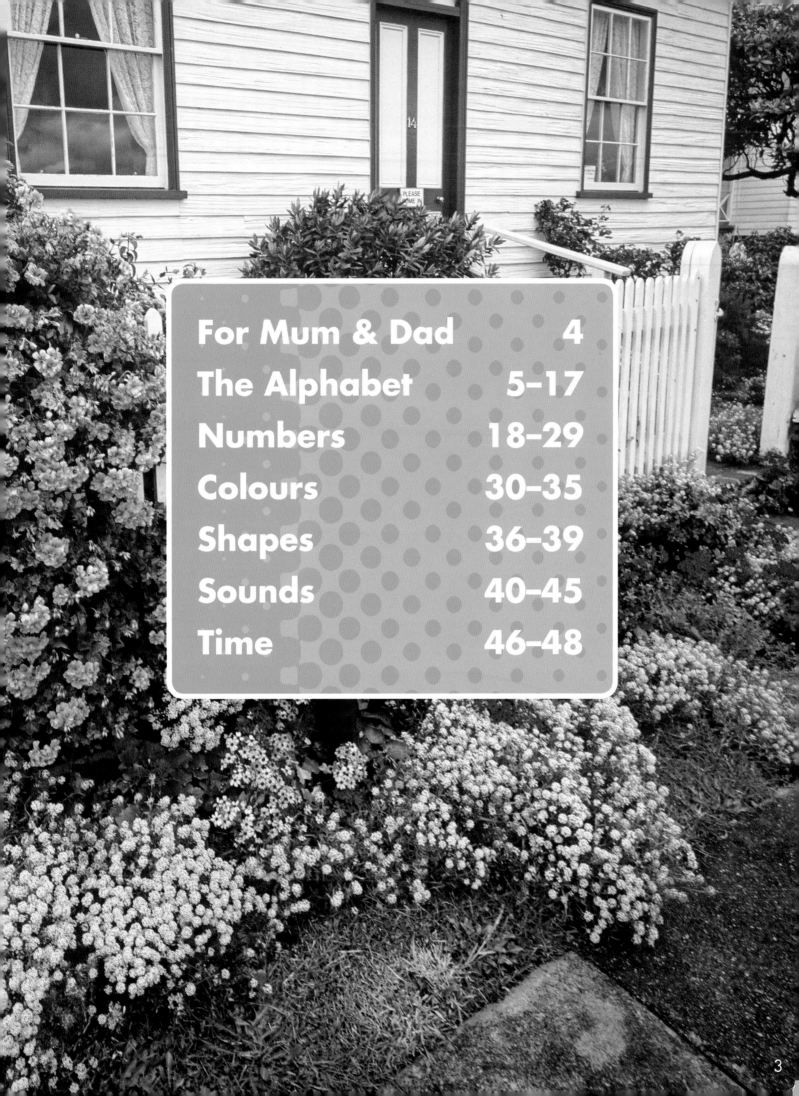

# How to use the alphabet pages ...

By allowing children to trace out each letter with their fingers, their brains receive and respond to multiple sensory inputs, reinforcing each letter's shape and relative size. Recognition and familiarity with the letter's shape is an essential prerequisite to articulating the letter sound.

As a precursor to writing, it is important that you follow the order of strokes identified for each letter. The starting point is particularly relevant and the child should start each letter at the point indicated (1) each time he or she encounters the letter. Along with speeding letter recognition, vital hand–eye co-ordination is enhanced.

Wherever possible, you should encourage your child to progress from the left-hand side of the page to the right, and from top to bottom, as you advance through the images. In other words, start with the capital on the left — then do the lower case equivalent on the right — before moving down to the next capital letter.

It is essential for children to master this left-to-right and top-to-bottom progression before reading and writing can become efficient.

# About numbers and counting ...

A child's understanding of numbers involves much more than just counting. Familiarity with the many different ways of representing numbers is one of the first steps in the learning process. Not only do children need to recognise the individual numerals, but they also need to develop a sense of quantity.

On each "number" page there are four ways of pictorially representing the number. Each page displays an image with a discrete number of items, a numeral (top left), a pattern of dots (top right) and finger representation (bottom left).

By including all these representations, children learn to recognise numerals while associating them with quantity, cardinality and order. As they re-use the book, the dot patterns in the top right of each page become useful too.

The dot patterns are organised in groups of three dots. By building familiarity with these patterns children eventually learn to *subitise* — a process whereby the brain instantly gauges a number without having to count each item.

As you can see, there is much more to counting than just knowing the names and the order of the numbers!

# The Alphabet

## With your pointer finger, trace the path each animal takes ...

Follow the ants as they travel down the left side of the hill. Then go back to the top and follow them down the right side.

Watch out! One of them has taken a short cut.

Bandicoots have been digging in my backyard. Can you see the holes they have left behind? Follow them with your pointer finger.

C c

The caterpillar is munching on the letter "C". He moves his head in a circle as he goes.

Use your finger to help him travel in the right direction.

Dogs like to smell the footprints of their friends to see where they have been.

Draw a nose on your finger and show the dog which way to go.

D d

This echidna wants to write the first letter of his common name. Show him which way to go. Use your finger to follow the arrows.

**E e**

Use you pointer finger to fly this flying-fox through the letter "F".

(Hanging upside down from a branch, flying-foxes first have to fall a short distance before they fly off.)

Fall from top to bottom before you fly across.

**F f**

This glider is ready to go gliding! Show it where to glide around the letter "G". The little "g" even looks like a glider, with a body and a tail.

A honeyeater is looking for food. Show it where to find the flowers filled with sweet nectar.

On the "H" don't forget to fly across home — remember to take your hat!

In my backyard the ibis flies steady and straight. Fly like the ibis — steady and straight.

The little "i" has a dot on top. Place the dot last of all.

Joey sometimes visits my backyard. She likes to jump around on the grass, but today Joey has lost her mum and needs your help to find her. Jump around the corner with Joey to help her find her mum.

This kangaroo is looking for her joey.

She will always start looking at the top and move down to the bottom. Help the kangaroo find her joey.

Draw an eye on your finger and go looking top to bottom.

Lorikeets climb into tree hollows. Follow the big lorikeet down the "L" hollow and around the bend.

Little lorikeet has found a hole that goes straight down the little "l".

Magpie is marching on the letter "M". March up and down, along with magpie.

"N" is for nocturnal and "N" is for night.

Nights are very dark in my backyard.

Take care moving along the "N" — it's hard to see at night!

It is still night-time in my backyard.

Oh, oh! The owls are out. They are flying around in circles. Catch them with your finger.

There is a playful possum living in my roof. He runs down the hall and around the kitchen looking for something to eat. Run your finger down and around to get to the food before the possum does!

The quolls are nesting in the letter "Q". Walk around the nest. Then show the baby quolls how to get out.

A rosella is resting on top of an "R". Race the rosella to the bottom. Return to the top and race it around the roses.

Snakes and skinks can sometimes look like the letter "S". Start at the top of the letter and run your finger around the bends towards the tail.

S s

A trail of termites runs from the top of a tree to its base and across it. Chase the termites down the "T" and across it with your finger.

T t

# U u

Ulysses is a butterfly that visits the flowers in my yard. It flutters down to land, lifts up and flutters down again.

Follow its flight path.

# V v

Vegetables grow in my garden. Animals that visit all agree vegetables are healthy foods to eat. Seeds are planted down in the soil and the plants grow up from there.

Willie wagtail wags his tail — down and up, down and up. Wag your finger through the letter "W" like the willie wagtail.

An "X" is in the word a**x**le — the middle of a wheel. Find the centre of the "x" where the two lines cross.

# Y y

Yellow is my favourite colour. Imagine putting on yellow gardening gloves and work your way around the letter "Y".

# Z z

Zoom along with zebra finch as she zips around the bends in the letter "Z".

# 1 Numbers

How many possums can you count on this log?

# 2

How many frogs can you see?

# 3

How many spades are there?

# 4

How many garden boots altogether?

# 5

How many feathers are here?

# 6

How many galahs in my backyard?
(Count them in twos.)

# 7

How many kangaroos are hopping through my backyard?

# 8

Count the butterflies that flitter in my garden ...

**9**

How many skinks are sunning themselves in my yard?

# 10

How many flowers are blooming in my garden?

# 0

**How many frogs can you see on the ferns?**

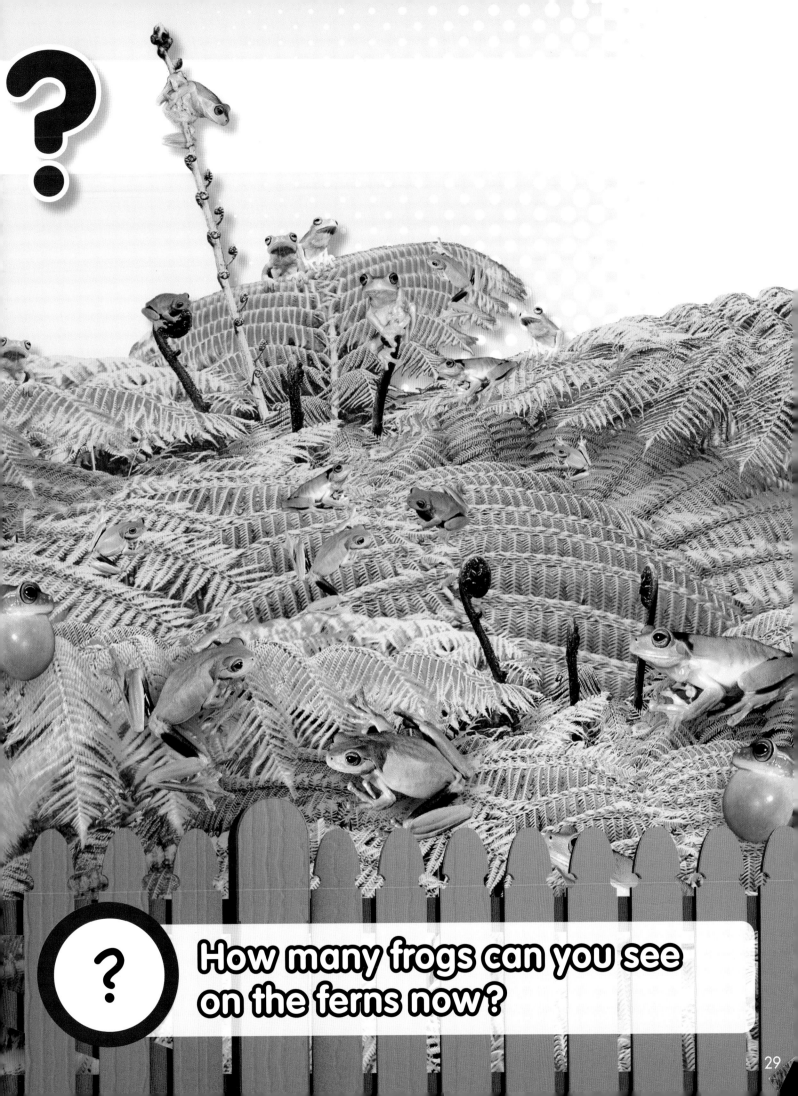

**?** How many frogs can you see on the ferns now?

# Colours

In my backyard I can see lots of different colours. What colours can you see?

**Green**

A green tree-frog

A scaly-breasted lorikeet with green feathers

# Red

A crimson rosella

My red spade

A red apple

31

# Blue

My wet weather boots and hat

A blue fairy-wren

**Flowers in my garden**

**My gardening gloves**

# orange

Parts of the hose are orange.

Oranges are orange!

Some flying-foxes have brown fur.

# Brown

Geckoes can change their colour.
This one is brown.

# Shapes

Find the circles in this picture ...

# Circles in nature

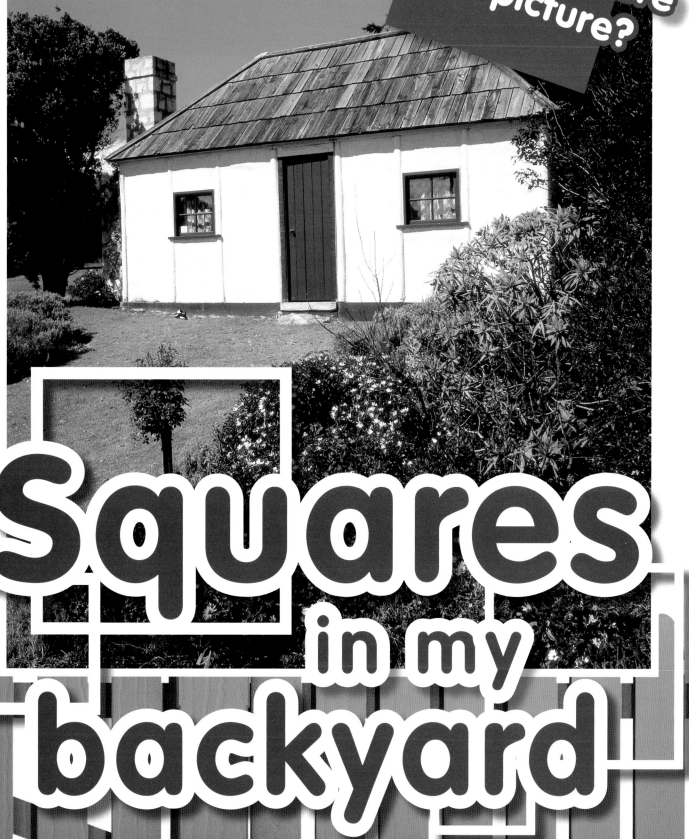

How many squares are there in this picture?

# Squares
## in my
## backyard

# Triangles
## on my roof

# Rectangles
## on my house

# Sounds

In my backyard I hear lots of different sounds. Do you know what animals make these sounds?

Sounds like a ...

Hisssss!

Quacks like a ...

Quack! Quack!

What makes this sound?

Chirp! Chirp! Chirp!

42

Who squeaked ?

# Squeak!

# Squeak!

# What did the cockatoo say?

# ¡Squawk!

What's making that noise in the drain pipe?

# Croak! Croak!

# Time

## Day Time

Parrots are diurnal, which means they are awake during the day.

Koalas are nocturnal — they sleep during the day.

# Night Time

Parrots are diurnal, which means they sleep at night.

Koalas are nocturnal — they are awake mostly at night.

# Bed Time

When is your bed time?
Are you nocturnal or diurnal?